Nature's
Wonders

BARRON'S

Alejandro Algarra / Gustavo Mazali

Contents

Birds are born from **eggs**

Did you know that before chicks hatch, their eggs provide all the food and water they need to survive? The parents take very good care of them. They take turns protecting them and keeping them warm so they can grow. When the chicks have eaten all the yolk and barely fit inside the egg anymore, they push with their legs, wings, and beak and . . . amazing! They are finally born!

Seven colors in the sky

What makes a rainbow? Sometimes, on rainy days, the sky clears up a bit and the sun's rays peek out from behind the clouds. If raindrops are still falling, the white light of the sun crosses through the rain. As the sun's rays go through each raindrop, they are divided into seven beautiful colors. An amazing rainbow is formed on the other side of the sky as thousands of raindrops are lit up by the sun, grouped into the seven colors.

From a **tadpole** to a frog

How do tadpoles become frogs? After they are born from their jelly-like eggs, tadpoles eat plants and breathe like fish. They keep growing as their legs gradually start to emerge, first the back ones and then the front ones. Their tails become shorter and they start to look less like a fish and more like a frog. They finally become frogs that jump out of the water, eat insects, and breathe with lungs, just like we do.

How snakes move

Snakes are reptiles. They are related to lizards, turtles, and crocodiles, yet they have no legs. So how do they get around? Their long bodies have lots of very powerful muscles, and they are covered with hundreds of scales.

Snakes move their muscles side to side as they grip their long belly scales into the ground. And that is how they move forward, slithering their bodies in S-shaped squiggles.

From tiny seeds to giant sequoias

Did you know that the largest
trees on our planet are born from
teeny tiny seeds? The tiny seed of the
sequoia tree has "wings" that help the wind carry
it. After just a few years, the sapling will measure dozens of
feet (meters) tall. With plenty of rain and a forest that is rich in plants,
fungus, and animals, and as long as fire and humans leave it alone,
a sequoia tree can actually reach more than 325 ft (100 m) tall and live
one or two thousand years.

13

A bird's
first flight

How do birds learn how to fly? They actually learn to fly
on their own. Just a few weeks after they are born, the
warm down that covers them is replaced by feathers.
This is when young chicks begin to flap their wings and
take tiny test leaps. Their parents stand near the nest
with food on a branch to encourage them to take flight.
After several attempts, the chicks fly from the nest, even
though no one has taught them how.

Tree rings

If you look at the trunk of a tree that has been cut down, you will see a lot of rings spreading out from the center to the bark. They tell the secret of a tree's age. As a tree trunk grows, only the part right under the bark is alive. In the spring and summer, the tree grows a lot and makes a thick ring. When the fall comes, it grows only a little and a thinner, darker ring is formed. If you count how many rings a tree trunk has, you can find out how many years the tree has been alive.

Plant food

How do plants eat? They use sunlight, air, water, and soil to make their food. The roots absorb water and salts from the soil, which reach the leaves by traveling through the stem. The air goes in and out of the leaves by tiny, invisible holes. With all of these ingredients (water, salts, and air) and with energy from the sun, the green parts of the plant make food, which the stem distributes around the entire plant.

19

Breathing
underwater

How do fish breathe? Instead of lungs, they have gills. If you look closely at a fish's head, you will see that there is a slit behind each eye. The gills are inside these slits. In sharks, there are several openings on each side of the body. Fish drink water and force it through their gills. Blood reaches the gills to absorb the oxygen, then the leftover water goes back out of the slits. Piece of cake!

Horse hooves

Can you imagine what it would be like to walk only on your tiptoes? Horses walk by supporting themselves on their middle fingers and toes. Their earliest ancestors were smaller and had all their fingers and toes. The next horses went from having five to three fingers and toes, and later they had just one on each hoof. On a horse's fingers and toes, the nails have become the hooves, which is what allows them to gallop at lightning speed.

Protective fur

What is fur for? Only mammals have fur, and this sets them apart from birds, reptiles, and amphibians. Fur covers their skin and is useful for many reasons.

The most important reason is to keep the body warm, but it also helps with the sense of touch. With some animals, the color of the fur serves as camouflage. And what do you think hedgehog and porcupine quills are made of? Fur!

Horns and antlers

Deer and reindeer have antlers. They are large with lots of points, and every year the antlers fall off, only to grow back the next year. The males use their antlers to fight and find out who is stronger. In contrast, cows, giraffes, mountain goats, and buffalo have real horns. These horns have bones inside that grow out of their head (skull), so they never fall off. The outside of the horns is covered with the same material as our fingernails.

Traveling **Seeds**

28

Plants make fruit with seeds inside. Plants cannot move, so how do they scatter their seeds? The seeds of some flowers, like dandelions, have tiny "umbrellas" that make them very light. If you blow hard, or when the wind blows, they fly off in all directions. The seeds of some trees, such as elm and maple, have wings: when a seed drops from the tree, the wings help it glide away.

29

Night flyers

Many animals fly by day when the sun is shining. Are there any that fly by night? Bats are mammals, just like you and me, but the amazing thing is that they have wings. Even though most people think bats can't see, they actually can see, but not well. So they manage to get around at night with their super sense of hearing. They hunt moths and mosquitos, which come out to fly after the sun goes down. Owls, which are birds, also hunt at night. They are guided by their huge eyes and sharp hearing.

From a caterpillar to a **butterfly**

How do caterpillars turn into butterflies? When they hatch from the egg, they are just tiny little worms that only think about one thing: food, food, and more food! Caterpillars spend every minute devouring leaves, flowers, and tender stems. When they get bigger, they change: they sit still and some of them wrap themselves in silk for protection. Once they are in the cocoon, they are called pupae. After some time, the pupa opens and what comes out? A beautiful butterfly!

Reef builders

Can an animal build a reef? On the bottom of the seas and oceans, there are thousands of tiny, almost invisible animals called coral. Each little coral critter makes a tiny stone house where it spends its entire life. When coral die, the animal disappears but the little house remains. Their children build their houses on top of their parents', and after hundreds and even thousands of years go by, these tiny houses, all piled together, form a coral reef.

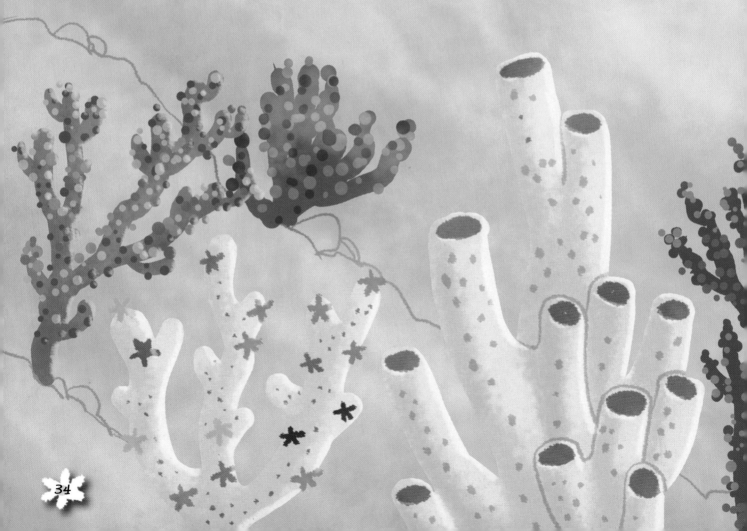

Luminous fish

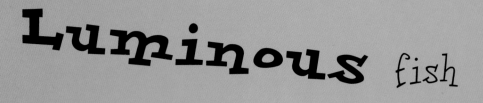

Can fish produce light? In the ocean, sunlight only reaches the upper part of the water. Seas and oceans can be very deep and completely dark near the bottom. Still, some deep-water fish can create their own light. They are animals with unusual shapes (huge eyes, long tails, sharp teeth) that use the light they make to communicate with each other. Some of them use it to distract predators and avoid being eaten, while others use it to attract and then eat other fish.

The best dads
in the world

How do seahorses make babies? When the time comes, the mother and father join their flexible tails and dance and connect their bodies. Then the female places her eggs in a little sack that the father has on his stomach, and he fertilizes the eggs with his seed. The eggs are protected and fed inside the sack. The little baby seahorses hatch from the eggs, and when they are big enough, the father releases them from his sack.

The journey of salmon

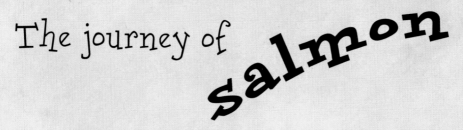

Why do salmon go back to the place where they were born? These fish are born in mountain rivers. They live in freshwater when they are young, but when they grow up, they swim down the river to reach the ocean. They keep growing and can travel very far to find food and other salmon. When the time comes, the largest ones return to the same river where they were born to lay their eggs, guided by the ocean currents and their sense of smell. Pretty smart!

Long-distance traveler **birds**

Why do some birds leave and come back the next year? Many types of birds spend the winters in warmer weather and come back to breed when the weather improves. Swallows, ducks, storks, and albatross are examples of birds that fly to warmer places when the cold settles in. Other birds never leave the places they live. For example, sparrows and crows live with us all year round, even when the winters are very harsh.

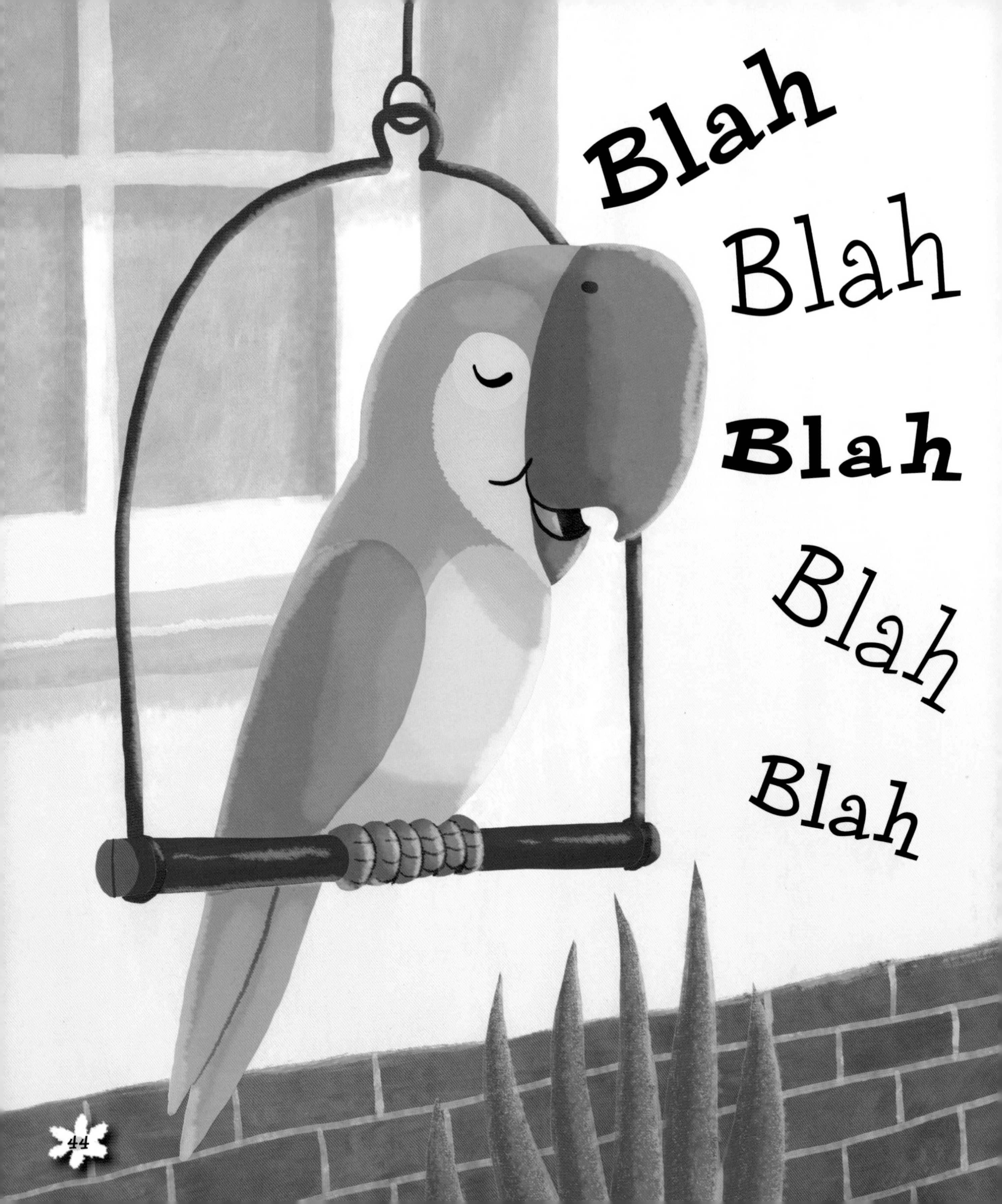
Blah
Blah
Blah
Blah
Blah

Talkative
birds

Have you ever heard a parrot talk? They are pretty smart birds. Thanks to the shape of their tongues and a special organ in their throats, they can imitate many sounds, including human language. They imitate their owners' words because these are the sounds they have heard since they were young, but yet they don't really know what they're saying. In nature, they will imitate the sounds of other birds to throw them off track, as well as communicate with other parrots and parakeets.

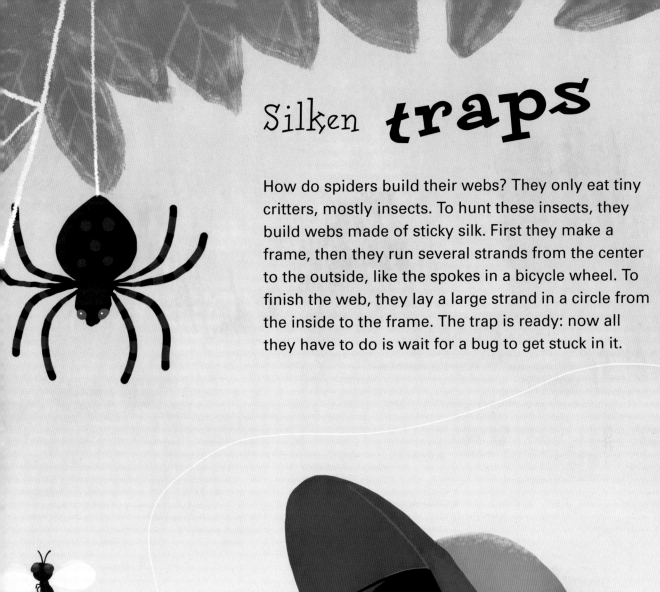

Silken traps

How do spiders build their webs? They only eat tiny critters, mostly insects. To hunt these insects, they build webs made of sticky silk. First they make a frame, then they run several strands from the center to the outside, like the spokes in a bicycle wheel. To finish the web, they lay a large strand in a circle from the inside to the frame. The trap is ready: now all they have to do is wait for a bug to get stuck in it.

Warm springs

Why are there some fountains and springs with very hot water? Earth's inside is warm, sometimes so warm that rocks are melted by the heat. A hot spring is formed when these melted rocks come in contact with water trapped underground. You can bathe in some of these hot springs, but other springs would be very dangerous to touch because the water is almost boiling.

Dew drops

How does dew form? It appears in the morning, especially at the end of summer. You can see a lot of tiny drops on blades of grass, spiderwebs, banisters, and cars that weren't there the night before. These drops don't come from rain. They appear because on clear, cloudless nights, the invisible water in the air turns into droplets that collect on cool surfaces.

51

A very peculiar mammal

Why is the platypus so incredible? In some ways, this Australian mammal is just like other mammals—it is covered in fur, it is warm-blooded, and it nurses its young. But unlike other mammals, it lays eggs! Also, its nose and feet are similar to those of a duck. In addition to all this, male platypuses are the only mammals that can make venom, like a snake. Amazing!

Lightning and thunder:
Storm

Sometimes, either before or during a storm, the sky lights up with a bright light called lightning. Soon after, we hear the deafening sound of thunder. What happened? Lightning is like a giant spark that travels from the clouds to the ground. This journey is very, very quick, so quick that as it travels down to the ground, the lightning actually splits the air in two. The thunder is the noise that this "spark" makes when it splits the air.

Carnivorous plants

Is it true that some plants are carnivorous? Plants usually get their food from the soil, but carnivorous plants live in very poor soil. In order to get a balanced diet, they will catch tiny bugs in their "traps." Some plants use sticky leaves, while others have jar-shaped leaves with a very slippery edge. Some even attract bugs with their colors and trap them between two leaves. Mmm, delicious!

A very powerful river

How was the Grand Canyon made? This impressive canyon is located in the state of Arizona. It is very long and has very deep walls. At the bottom of the canyon is the Colorado River. Millions of years ago, the land was actually flat. Gradually, year after year, the river chipped away tiny pieces of rock and carried them out to sea, carving out the Grand Canyon as we now know it.

A special garden

If we look at the animals that inhabit the bottom of warm, shallow waters, we can find many different types without going very deep: Beautiful starfish, sea urchins with their spines, brightly colored coral that sometimes carpet the rocks and other times grow like huge branches of a tree, sea anemones with long tentacles, and feathery duster worms and their tube-shaped homes.

Claws
on the feet

Claws are found at the tip of the feet in birds, reptiles, and mammals. They are made of the same material as fur and feathers, and when they grow they can become sharp. Birds use them to run (such as an ostrich), to grab things, and to hold themselves steady on branches. Birds of prey also use their claws to hunt. Reptiles use them to move along the ground, and both mammals and reptiles use them to hunt, grab, and climb.

Traveling pollen

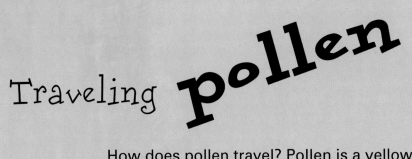

How does pollen travel? Pollen is a yellowish powder that is produced by the stamens of a flower. In order for a flower to become a fruit with seeds, it has to be pollinated by another flower. Some flowers are brightly colored, rich in nectar, and smell sweet, so they attract insects, birds, and other animals. When the animals drink the nectar, they carry the pollen that sticks to them to another flower. Other flowers, like those from pine and fir trees, just let the wind carry the pollen off.

Living in the desert

How do plants and animals live in the desert? The desert is a place where life has to adapt to survive. By day, the heat is unbearable and by night it is extremely cold, plus there is hardly any water because it almost never rains. Plants like cacti can store water in their stems. The leaves have turned into thorns to make sure that the desert animals don't steal their treasure. Many animals spend the day hidden in their dens or under rocks, and they only come out in early morning or at night.

The cricket's song

Have you ever heard crickets chirping a loud song? Think of the sounds of warm summer nights. Do you know how and why they sing? Only the males can, and they sing to attract females, as well as to keep other males away. They don't use their voices to sing, as birds and humans do. Instead, they use their wings. Each wing has tiny wrinkles and bulges, which make a chirping sound when they are rubbed together.

Chirp *Chirp* **Chirp**

The dance of the fireflies

Have you ever seen a field lit up by fireflies? It is one of the most beautiful displays in nature. When night falls, you can see their tiny lights flickering on and off. They light up the meadow, the flowers, the bushes, and the tree branches. All fireflies make light, young and old alike. The young ones use it to warn predators about their sour taste (yuck!), while the adult fireflies light up to attract a partner.

A beaver's work

There are few mammals as hardworking as beavers. When these rodents choose a spot on the river to build their home, they get straight to work. They use their long teeth to saw off branches and trees, and use their wide, strong tails to carry the wood to the river. Then they stack the wood to make a dam. The little "lake" the dam creates forms a den, where the beavers can live safely with their families.

Living on the ice

Polar bears live in the North Pole, and emperor penguins live in the South Pole. Both places are extremely cold all year round. To survive in the cold, both animals have a very thick layer of fat under their skin. Polar bears have very dense white fur that keeps them warm and helps them blend in with the ice and snow. Penguins gather together in large groups and take turns with their fellow penguins huddling in the inside of the circle in order to stay warm.

It's not a plant,
but it's not an animal

Are fungi plants or animals? Fungi are living beings, but they are neither plants nor animals. In the past, people believed that they were a rare kind of plant. Many fungi live underground near the roots of trees and are invisible to the human eye. When the time comes to grow and multiply, fungi create a mushroom that pops out of the soil or springs up on tree trunks. The spores are inside these mushrooms, like the "seeds" of the new fungi.

A vegetarian, pajama-wearing **bear**

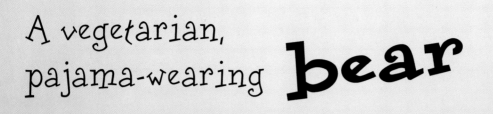

Why is the panda so different from other bears? First, it is black around the eyes, snout, ears, and the feet, while the rest of its body is white. Panda food is also very special, since they only eat bamboo—they can eat up to 90 lbs (40 kg) per day! Did you know that this giant, solitary, peaceful bear from the forests of China has six toes on its front feet? The extra toe is like a thumb that helps hold the bamboo branches.

Unstoppable ants

Where do ants get their power? They are tiny insects that have managed to conquer our entire planet. Teamwork with fellow ants allows them to be successful and strong, despite their size. There is a queen in every anthill; she is the mother of hundreds or even thousands of worker ants. They all work together in the anthill to take care of the queen, bring food, explore new places, and protect against attacks. All for one and one for all!

Sleeping *to handle the cold*

Why do some animals hibernate? Many animals, both large and small, sleep as a way to get through the winter. The brown bear, the squirrel, and the marmot sleep for several months when winter is at its coldest. They prepare themselves in the fall by eating a lot so they can survive without food when snow blankets the ground. In cold places, snakes, turtles, and frogs also seek shelter and don't come out again until the spring. Did you know that many insects also bury themselves underground to hibernate?

Dense jungles

In the jungle, trees grow to great heights. Their trunks are covered with climbing plants, ivy, and flowers, such as orchids. This means that hardly any light reaches the ground. There are snakes, monkeys, sloths, frogs, birds, and many other animals that live far out of sight in the upper reaches or canopies of the trees, where they find food, rainwater, and light.

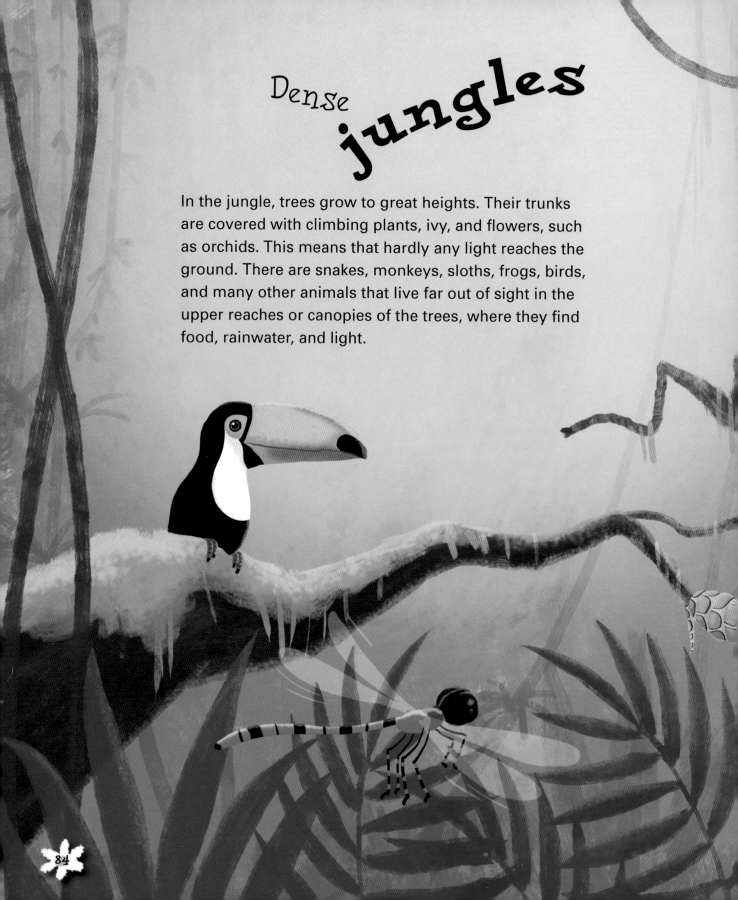

Same problem, same solution

Did you know that hippopotamuses, crocodiles, and frogs are similar? They are very different animals, but all three spend a lot of time in the water. In order for them to stay underwater but still be able to see and breathe, they all have reached the same solution: their eyes and nostrils are on top of their heads. Pretty ingenious!!

Living inside a **shell**

Why do turtles have shells? They weigh them down and prevent them from running or moving quickly like lizards and snakes. But there is one major advantage to having a shell: most animals cannot attack turtles because their shell is so hard. When they are in danger, some of them can completely hide their heads, legs, and tail inside the shell. It's almost like they're saying: "No one comes into my house!"

Walking
on your belly

If you look closely at cute little snails, you'll notice that they are very unique animals. The shells they carry on their backs give them protection and a place to hide while they sleep. Their eyes are on the tip of a pair of long tentacles that stick out of their heads, while another pair of smaller tentacles are used to feel what's around them. The strangest thing about snails might be the way they walk. They don't have feet or legs! They slide along on their bellies, leaving behind a trail of slime to help them move. "Goodbye, Mr. Snail!"

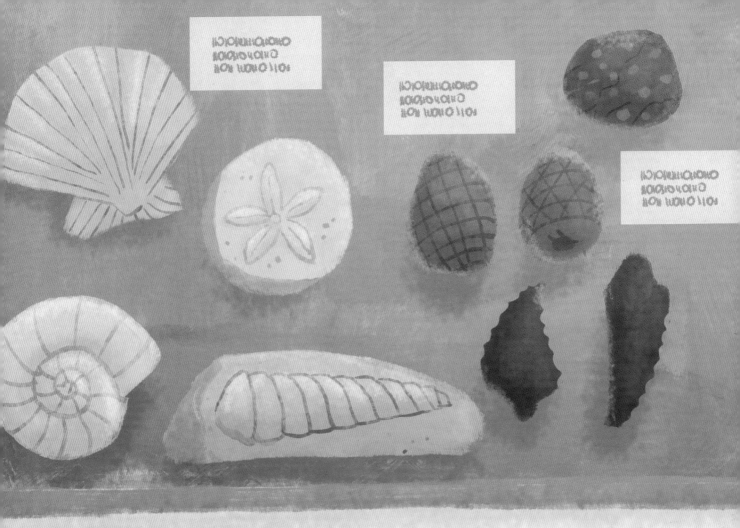

Stones that used to be plants and animals

What is a fossil? You may have found a stone that looked like a shell or a snail, or maybe it had the imprint of a sea creature. While they may be stones now, thousands and thousands of years ago they were actual living things. Sometimes, when these living things die, the harder part of the animal, such as the teeth, bones, shells, and spine, will turn to stone. Wood and leaves can turn into fossils as well, and can last for a very long time.

Dolphins and whales

Even though dolphins and whales look like fish, they are mammals, just like us. To live in the water, their front legs turned into fins, and their back legs adapted to a very strong tail. Their skin isn't covered with fur, which makes them glide through the water more easily. Dolphins, sperm whales, and orcas eat fish and squid. Other whales, however, eat huge amounts of tiny crustaceans called krill.

Nature's
Wonders

First edition for the United States and Canada published in 2018 by Barron's Educational Series, Inc.

Original title of the book in Spanish:
MARAVILLAS DE LA NATURALEZA
© Copyright GEMSER PUBLICATIONS S.L., 2017
C/ Castell, 38; Teiá (08329) Barcelona, Spain
(World Rights)
Tel: 93 540 13 53
E-mail: *info@mercedesros.com*
Website: *www.mercedesros.com*
Author: Alejandro Algarra
Illustrator: Gustavo Mazali

All inquiries should be addressed to:
Barron's Educational Series, Inc.
250 Wireless Boulevard
Hauppauge, NY 11788
www.barronseduc.com

Library of Congress Control Number:
2017948460
ISBN: 978-1-4380-1096-0

Date of Manufacture: January 2018
Manufactured by: L. Rex Printing
Company Limited, Dongguan, China

Printed in China
9 8 7 6 5 4 3 2 1